For Glen + Nancy
Blessings and Peace!
Adam L. Tice
June 14, 2004

MW01318618

Woven Into Harmony

50 Hymn Texts

by

Adam M. L. Tice

GIA Publications, Inc. 7404 S. Mason Ave., Chicago, Illinois 60638
1-800-GIA-1358 • (708) 496-3800 • www.giamusic.com

Publisher's Note

The publication of this edition is intended to make available some of the collected hymn texts of Adam Tice. It is our hope that this volume will be useful to worship leaders and church musicians, and of special interest to hymnal editors and tune writers.

Each text is first presented in poetic form, and then interlined with either an existing or newly composed tune. It is not our intent, however, that the singing of these texts be limited to the tunes with which they appear in this collection. Composers are invited to fashion new melodies to carry these words.

GIA is dedicated to the work of this writer, and this publication represents a desire to introduce his work to the larger community. We are committed to simplifying the process by which individuals and congregations are able to use these hymns in their own work and worship. For non-commercial permission to reproduce the texts or tunes of these hymns, contact OneLicense.net or the individual copyright holders. GIA will make the hymns in this collection available through HymnPrint.net, an online service providing downloadable files for worship bulletins.

Notice

The unauthorized copying of the *words* or *music* of this edition, for any reason whatsoever, is a direct violation of the copyright law for which the person responsible, as well as the institution he or she represents, is subject to prosecution. This includes hand copying, photo copying, even the making of just one copy. To do so is to deprive the persons whose names appear in this edition, as well as the publisher and its employees, of just income.

ISBN 13: 978-1-57999-762-5

Woven into Harmony
Cover design and illustration by Rosanna McFadden
Copyright © 2009 by GIA Publications, Inc.
7404 S. Mason Ave., Chicago, IL 60638 USA
www.giamusic.com
International Copyright Secured
All Rights Reserved
Printed in the USA.

Contents

Foreword 4
Biography 5
Preface 6
A Woman Poured Her Jar of Rich Perfume 8
An Echo of the Voice of God 10
As the Birds of the Air 12
At the Pulpit, Font, and Table 14
Away in a Manger 16
beyond 18
Breath of God, Breath of Peace 20
Christ Is for Losers 23
Christ, the Victorious 26
Come, Join in Mary's Prophet-song 28
Coming Together for Wine and for Bread 31
Creation Is Not Built Upon 34
Earth Is Full of Wit and Wisdom 36
Every Eye Is Different 38
Fill Us with Your Breath 40
God Bestows on Every Sense 42
God, Bless the Doctor's Art 43
God, Grant This Suffering Soul Release 44
God, in Our Praying 46
God of Music, Guide Our Song 49
God Says, "I Give My Earth to You" 50
God, Your Knowing Eye Can See 52
I AM the Living Water 54
"I Have No Room" 57
In Floods of Chaos 60
In the Darkness of the Morning 62
Jesus Entered Egypt 64

Jesus Promises Communion 66
Jesus Said to Pray, "Our Father" 68
Jesus, Show Us How to Pray 70
On the Sabbath Day of Rest 72
Open Your Eyes to the Image of God 74
"Peace Be with You!" 76
She Moves Where She Wishes 78
The Church of Christ Cannot Be Bound 80
The Dazzle of Diamonds 82
The First One to Know 85
The Spirit Is a Dove 88
The Strong and Gentle Voice 90
The World at Day's Dawn 92
This Dreadful Cross 94
We Dream of a Turning 96
What Comfort Can Our Worship Bring 98
What New Endeavors Will We Dare 101
When Anyone Can Buy a Gun 104
When Jesus Learned His Friend Had Died . . 106
When Job the Great Was Brought to Tears . . 108
When My Soul Is Sore and Troubled 110
Who Follows Jesus? 112
Who Is This Who Breaches Borders 114
Scriptural Index 116
Liturgical and Topical Index 120
Index of Composers and Sources 123
Metrical Index 124
Tune Index 125
Title and First Line Index 126

Foreword

For the past several years I have had the pleasure of occasionally discovering among my incoming e-mails new hymn texts from Adam Tice. I always read them with much anticipation because I have learned to expect good things from him, and readers of the fifty hymns collected here will soon find out why.

While a collection of hymns does not attempt to sustain a plot line like that of a mystery novel, I feel something akin to such a reviewer's obligation not to give away too much in these introductory remarks. A significant part of the pleasure of discovering new hymns is finding how they give voice to a concern, an insight, a juxtaposition, a hope, a memory, a tension, or some other feature that has somehow been omitted in other hymns. Many such discoveries lie ahead in this volume.

One way of appreciating Adam's gifts as a hymnwriter is to keep in mind that he comes to the craft of text writing from his experience as a songleader in a tradition that primarily sings unaccompanied and in parts. Sensitivity to the pacing and pitching of singers carries over to a keen sense of the sonic aspects of his texts, especially in alliteration, assonance, and rhyme. Because these devices are used gracefully and unobtrusively, they add conviction and assurance to the texts rather than interrupting the flow of ideas. Similarly, to be an effective songleader, one needs a clear awareness of one's own voice, and Adam has developed a comparable consciousness of the language that comes naturally to him. On more than one occasion when he has sent me a first draft of a new text, he has declined to use my hints for alternative words or phrases when they were not "something I would say." But then he would recast the line or stanza in his own idiom and produce something more coherent than my piecemeal suggestion.

There are numerous words and phrases in these hymns that definitely move beyond traditional hymnic vocabulary, but they are not inserted irresponsibly or for sheer shock value. On the contrary, they often evoke a response such as "Why have I never seen this word in a hymn before?" Admittedly, there are a few instances—such as a text involving both "gecko" and "sea slug"—that are intentionally lighthearted in the expansion of hymnic diction, but there are others that are breathtaking in their unflinching immediacy: "Christ is for losers," "When anyone can buy a gun," "we slash and burn and pave." Yet whether amusing or challenging or meditative or narrative or anything else, the very variety and range of the language ultimately contributes to a sense that these hymns merit careful attention.

Comparable to this breadth of vocabulary is the diversity of the metrical forms in which these hymns are cast. The fifty hymns in this collection employ no less than thirty-five distinct meters, several of which are not found in most hymnals. Yet the technical challenge never becomes the central concern of the text. Instead, it operates as a means of enhancing the intent of the hymn and gives life to lines that could well have become pedestrian in more familiar meters.

Because some of the tunes selected to carry these texts are well known from other hymns, the associations with previous texts often intensify the experience of singing the new pairings that appear in this volume. The incarnational connotations of CRANHAM, for example, add poignancy to a text about enlarging our sense of the range of human differences. In other cases, the incorporation of tunes usually regarded as secular serves as a reminder that the whole of life is within God's keeping and deserves attention in our sung prayer. Operating in a slightly different way, the retrieval of unfamiliar tunes, such as the sturdy, Welsh LLEDROD, gives depth and energy to new words. And the constant unfolding and growing of congregational song is evident in the tunes by living composers that either inspired or were inspired by the texts appearing here.

As I hope these introductory comments will indicate, Adam Tice has brought together here a remarkable first collection of hymns deserving attention and use. They leave one both grateful and eager for more.

—Carl P. Daw, Jr.
Executive Director
The Hymn Society in the United States and Canada

Biographical Sketch

Adam M. L. Tice was born on October 11, 1979, in the mountains of western Pennsylvania, and grew up in Alabama, Oregon, and Indiana. After graduating from high school in Elkhart, Indiana, Adam went to nearby Goshen College, a Mennonite liberal arts school. He majored in music with an emphasis on composition and completed a minor in Bible and religion, graduating in 2002. He began working as a church musician and choir director while still in college.

Adam took his first course at the Associated Mennonite Biblical Seminary in the fall of 2003, which led to the writing of his initial hymn text. Four years later (including a year-long interlude as a full time marionette puppeteer), Adam graduated with a Master of the Arts in Christian Formation with an emphasis on worship. He completed a thesis on the life of Jesus as presented in Mennonite hymnals of the twentieth century. *The Conrad Grebel Review* published his research into ways that hymnody shaped the Mennonite practices of communion.

He has led singing at numerous Mennonite and ecumenical events, including the 2008 Hymn Sing for Peace on the steps of the United States Capitol reflecting pool.

Adam was the winner of the tenth annual Macalester Plymouth United Church (St. Paul, Minnesota) hymn competition. *More Voices*, a hymn supplement for the United Church of Canada, was the first major collection to include one of his texts ("Breath of God, Breath of Peace"). Adam is a member of the Executive Committee of The Hymn Society in the United States and Canada.

In November of 2007, Adam and his wife María moved to the Washington, DC, suburbs, where Adam was installed as Associate Pastor of Hyattsville Mennonite Church in Hyattsville, Maryland.

Preface

There is something disconcerting about writing this preface. As a student in seminary and as a beginning hymn writer, I have read paragraphs like these in order to glean wisdom about process and inspiration. The insecure part of me would suggest that the reader stop here and pick up a collection by a more seasoned writer. Read their forewords and find words of wisdom. Learn from Daw, Dufner, Bringle, Bell, Troeger, and Kaan, as I did. They will tell you how a hymn is written. Their prefaces introduce this work as well because their craft informed and inspired mine. But I will set aside my insecurity and tell my story. After all, each of the writers whom I admire once put together a first collection and wrote a first preface.

It seems that every hymn writer has a moment of revelation, where for some reason or another they fit words together in this form for the first time. My epiphany came as an assignment in my first seminary course, "Congregational Song: Practices Past and Present." Professor Rebecca Slough asked us to pick a favorite psalm and write a metrical version. We were to spend a maximum of thirty minutes on our text, lest we found it so challenging that it absorb an inordinate amount of time. My experience was surprisingly satisfying. The components of meter and rhyme provided a framework for poetic expressions of spirituality. Refining sentences and images into short poetic lines and stanzas becomes a sort of theological crossword puzzle. For most people, that combination of elements is horribly constraining. But for hymn writers the combination is strangely liberating. I tried my hand at several more texts, retelling the stories of Jesus as hymns. One of those early efforts, "When Jesus Learned His Friend Had Died," appears in this collection.

As Prof. Slough describes it, a floodgate was opened. I found my voice in the intricacies of the hymn form. I wrote at a fierce pace and within a year had produced some thirty-six hymns. Trained as a musician and immersed in the Mennonite singing tradition, I already saw my vocation as enabling the voice of congregations. Now I found myself giving words to those voices. The Associated Mennonite Biblical Seminary (Elkhart, Indiana) and Bethel Missionary Church (Goshen, Indiana) were willing proving grounds for the new hymns. Many of the texts I wrote were for specific worship services at those two communities, while others were responses to lectures or sermons.

Finding the right word, the appropriate register of language, and just the right rhythm for a particular theme inspires me to test and refine my spirituality and theology. A rhyming dictionary will suggest a connection that I might not find in a theological textbook. A melodic arch will require me to identify the core of the idea I am processing. The constraints of the form actually free me to discover subtle nuances that I would miss in writing a sermon on the same topic.

In the summer of 2004, less than a year after writing my first text, I experienced my first conference of The Hymn Society in the United States and Canada. I attended as a Lovelace Scholar and was star-struck from the start. I began meeting people whose hymns I had sung, studied, and loved, and found these luminaries to be remarkably down to earth, friendly, and generous. Since that time, many Hymn Society members have provided helpful critique and advice. Executive Director Carl Daw, who was already my favorite living hymn writer, deserves particular mention for his invaluable feedback.

During that first conference I was paired with a roommate from Illinois named Chris Ángel. I gave him copies of my work the first day, and he began composing tunes for them by the second day. The parish he served, St. Patrick's Catholic Church in Urbana, was the first congregation to sing a number of the texts by this Mennonite writer. One of my great joys in the publication of this collection is the inclusion of five of Chris' tunes. These are his first published compositions.

Thanks to my Mennonite background, I am partial to tunes that can be sung *a cappella* and in parts; however, I enjoy and appreciate a wide variety of music, from chant, to folk, to rock. While I believe that the tunes provided in this collection will prove useful, they should not be considered the final word. Church musicians and editors should feel free to experiment with different pairings according to the needs of their communities. I especially hope that this publication will inspire the work of additional composers.

Further pieces of this story will emerge as part of the commentary on individual hymns throughout the collection. I have been amazed and humbled that my words have served their purpose in communities of faith across the United States and Canada. I began writing in an attempt to fill a perceived void in Mennonite hymnals. We have traditionally sung very few hymns by Mennonite writers, and as a result we are shaped primarily by borrowed theology. I wanted to give voice to the unique contributions of our theology and to offer those gifts to the wider church. I hope that these hymns can express our shared longing for peace and justice, reconciliation, and the unfolding of the new creation.

I acknowledge and thank:
- —the teachers who have shaped me musically and in other ways: Carol Nelson, Dennis Phipps, Doyle Preheim, Lee Dengler, Mary K. Oyer, and Rebecca Slough;
- —the innumerable Hymn Society friends and mentors who have encouraged me;
- —the people at GIA Publications, especially Randall Sensmeier, who developed this project with an expert editorial touch and graciousness;
- —Rosanna McFadden for providing the tree image for the cover of this collection;
- —Chris Ángel, Randall Sensmeier, Sally Ann Morris, and Ronald Krisman for tunes written specifically for this collection, as well as the numerous other composers who have granted permission for their works to appear here;
- —the communities of faith that have nurtured my writing and tested the results: Bethel Missionary Church, Associated Mennonite Biblical Seminary, and Hyattsville Mennonite Church;
- —my parents, Ezra and Joan Tice;
- —my most honest critic and beloved companion in life, María Celesta Longoria Tice.

—Adam M. L. Tice

A Woman Poured Her Jar of Rich Perfume

Meter: 10 10 10 10

A woman poured her jar of rich perfume
  all over Jesus' feet with loving care.
She knelt as fragrance quickly filled the room.
  She washed his feet, and wiped them with her hair.

She washed his feet, not thinking of the cost;
  the best she had the woman freely gave.
His love was more to her than money lost.
  Her gift anointed Jesus for his grave.

Text: Adam M. L. Tice, 2004; © 2009, GIA Publications, Inc.

This hymn depicts the intimate exchange described in John 12:1–7. The practice of footwashing, recently revived in many churches, is an important expression of Christian servanthood and love.

Text: Adam M. L. Tice, 2004; © 2009, GIA Publications, Inc.
Tune: SURSUM CORDA; Alfred M. Smith, 1879–1971; © 1941, Episcopal Church of the Ascension, Atlantic City, NJ

An Echo of the Voice of God

Meter: 9 11

Hum

This cry, this groan, this psalm pouring out,
pouring out, an echo of the voice of God.

Hum

This chant, this hum, this song rising up,
rising up, an echo of the voice of God.

Hum

This hush, this rest, this prayer, soft and still,
soft and still, an echo of the voice of God.

Hum

Text: Adam M. L. Tice, 2007; © 2009, GIA Publications, Inc.

Physicists tell us that the sound of the "big bang" is still detectable in space. In fact, no sound has a stopping point; it simply drops below the level of human hearing and drifts into space. The entire universe, then, carries the voice of God—the infinite expression of "Let there be…." Our own prayers and songs are an echo of that voice. At the 2008 conference of The Hymn Society in the United States and Canada held in Berkeley, California, Mary Louise Bringle suggested WADA as a name for Sally Ann Morris' tune. Wada is the residence hall on the University of California campus where many conference attendees stayed.

11

* "Swing" eighth notes except where indicated otherwise.

Text: Adam M. L. Tice, 2007; © 2009 GIA Publications, Inc.
Tune: WADA TUNE; Sally Ann Morris, b. 1952; © 2009, GIA Publications, Inc.

As the Birds of the Air

Meter: 66 9 D

As the birds of the air
trust in God for their care
  without fear, for they know they will feed,
so in faith we should trust,
knowing God will be just,
  and provide us with all that we need.

What we need, Jesus knows:
things to eat, shelter, clothes,
  human touch, fearless love, and good friends.
When he walked here on earth
and took part in our birth,
  he relied on the gifts that God sends.

Even still, there remain
people lost in their pain:
  needing food, dry with thirst, all alone.
And does God just ignore
all the grief of the poor?
  Who will hear when we weep, wail, or groan?

And yet, God has supplied
enough goods to divide
  if we turn from our fear, hate, and greed.
We can answer a prayer
with our love, grace, and care,
  and through us God can meet ev'ry need.

Text: Adam M. L. Tice, 2004; © 2009, GIA Publications, Inc.

Alternate tunes include Dan Damon's "like a child," EXULTATION, and NEW CONCORD. If, as Jesus instructed, we are not to worry about tomorrow, what do we do with the reality of suffering? It is our responsibility to do what we can to meet the needs of others. The opening phrase of the tune used here suggests a bird's song to me. Chris Ángel named the tune for the state bird of both Indiana and Illinois, our respective places of residence at the time.

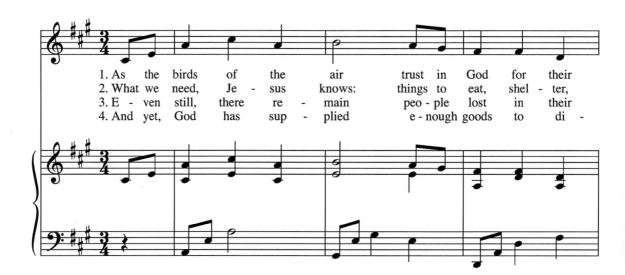

Text: Adam M. L. Tice, 2004; © 2009, GIA Publications, Inc.
Tune: CARDINAL; Chris Ángel, b. 1976; © 2009, GIA Publications, Inc.

At the Pulpit, Font, and Table

Meter: 8 7 8 7 8 7

At the pulpit, font, and table,
  named by God to serve and lead
in the priesthood lived by Jesus,
  summoned to a people's need,
sister*, as God's Spirit calls you,
  answer with each word and deed.

Once you felt baptismal waters;
  you have shared the bread and wine.
You have heard the songs and sermons;
  you have studied Word and sign.
Through these gifts that God has given
  earth and heaven intertwine.

*"brother" or "servant" may be used

Taste and see that God dwells with you;
  hear God's voice in song and prayer.
Lead into the unknown spaces;
  find that God is always there.
Offer healing hands for comfort
  and receive the Spirit's care.

God, you call us all to service,
  naming each of us a priest.
You desire our acts of justice:
  mercy for the lost and least.
Humbly, we would walk with Jesus,
  calling guests to join his feast.

Text: Adam M. L. Tice, 2007; © 2009, GIA Publications, Inc.

I wrote this text for the ordination of a Hymn Society friend, Anissa Bacon—note the acrostic in stanza one. It is offered as a reflection on preparation for ministry, the roles of a pastor, and the common call to ministry of all Christians. PICARDY is an effective alternate tune.

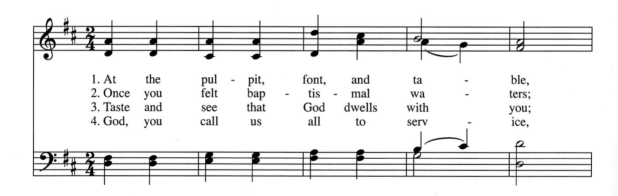

*"brother" or "servant" may be used

Text: Adam M. L. Tice, 2007; © 2009 GIA Publications, Inc.
Tune: LAUDA ANIMA; John Goss, 1800–1880

Away in a Manger

Meter: 11 11 11 11

Away in a manger, no crib for a bed,
dear Mary and Joseph lay Jesus' sweet head.
  The stars with their shimmering songs fill the sky
  to sing their Creator his first lullaby.

The cattle are mooing; the poor baby cries
as Joseph, exhausted, wipes tears from his eyes.
  And Mary looks down on the face of her son:
  the infant in whom our new life is begun.

How wondrous the myst'ry that God comes to earth,
where animals witness the pain of his birth.
  A Bethlehem stable is home for the night
  for Jesus, our star, our salvation, our light.

Text: Adam M. L. Tice, 2006; © 2009, GIA Publications, Inc.

The commonly used version of this beloved carol makes many theologians cringe with its depiction of Jesus. In it, the newborn Jesus lays down his own head and doesn't cry at all. In short, the Jesus depicted is not a real human. However, Jesus arrived just like the rest of us. He needed parents to tuck him in at night. He cried. This is part of the mystery of the incarnation—that God was fully human. The third verse is inspired by the Latin text "O magnum mysterium." Associated Mennonite Biblical Seminary professor Daniel Schipani prompted this revision.

Text: Adam M. L. Tice, 2006; © 2009, GIA Publications, Inc.
Tune: AFTON WATER; Scottish traditional

beyond

Meter: 6 6 6 4

beyond the bounds of space
 beyond the universe
  beyond the farthest star
God sings "I AM"

beyond the bounds of time
 beyond eternity
  beyond all life and death
God sings "I AM"

beyond the bounds of mind
 beyond the intellect
  beyond all human thought
God sings "I AM"

within this storied place
 within the here and now
  within our fellowship
God sings "I AM"

Text: Adam M. L. Tice, 2005; © 2009, GIA Publications, Inc.

This tune may be sung unaccompanied as a canon, with voices entering at the end of the first or second full measures. The omission of capitalization and punctuation is designed to suggest a continuous sound with no beginning or ending. I was inspired to write in this form by Dan Damon's "like a child."

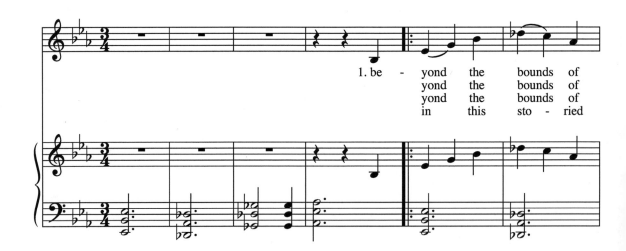

Text: Adam M. L. Tice, 2005; © 2009, GIA Publications, Inc.
Tune: TRANSCENDENT; Chris Ángel, b. 1976; arr. Randall Sensmeier, b. 1948; © 2009, GIA Publications, Inc.

Breath of God, Breath of Peace

Meter: Irregular

Breath of God, Breath of peace,
Breath of love, Breath of life,
Breath of justice, Breath of passion,
Breath creating, Breath of healing,
Breath of singing, Breath of praying,

Come upon us,
come restore us,
come inspire us,
Breath of God.

Word of God, Word of peace,
Word of love, Word of life,
Word of justice, Word of passion,
Word creating, Word of healing,
Word of singing, Word of praying,

Come upon us,
come restore us,
come inspire us,
Word of God.

Voice of God, Voice of peace,
Voice of love, Voice of life,
Voice of justice, Voice of passion,
Voice creating, Voice of healing,
Voice of singing, Voice of praying,

Come upon us,
come restore us,
come inspire us,
Voice of God.

Text: Adam M. L. Tice, 2004; © 2009, GIA Publications, Inc.

This was my first attempt at a non-traditional form, and the first of my texts to be included in a hymn collection. It appears in *More Voices*, a United Church of Canada hymnal supplement, published in 2007. When I avoid rhyme and traditional meter, I rely upon other features as a source of structure, particularly repetition. I followed the example of Jaroslav Vajda's "Now the Silence" in setting up a repeating and predictable sequence of simple phrases. Breath, Word, and Voice are common Biblical images that, when combined, become an image of the Trinity.

Text: Adam M. L. Tice, 2004; © 2009 GIA Publications, Inc.
Tune: PATTERNS; Sally Ann Morris, b. 1952; © 2009, GIA Publications, Inc.

Christ Is for Losers

Meter: 10 10 10 11 with refrain

Christ is for losers, the last, and the least,
welcoming sinners and saints to his feast,
  turning away those who bring their own bread—
  all those who assume they don't need to be fed.

  REFRAIN:
  All my loss I count as gain,
    all of my weakness, all of my pain.
      And though I die, with Christ I will rise,
      for life is in Christ, the loser's prize.

Christ is for losers, the homeless, the poor,
jobless and hopeless who knock at his door.
  Christ won't admit those who bring their own key,
  who lock up the Church that Christ calls to be free. *Refrain*

Christ is for losers, the broken and ill,
lacking insurance to cover their bill.
  Those who don't know they need healing at all
  will pay no attention to Christ and his call. *Refrain*

Christ is for losers, the wand'ring, the lost,
those called "illegal" for lines they have crossed.
  Christ unites people divided by hate
  and crosses the borders earth's powers create. *Refrain*

Text: Adam M. L. Tice, 2006; © 2009, GIA Publications, Inc.

The Rev. Matt Yoder at Bethel Missionary Church in Goshen, Indiana, preached a sermon that he called "The Kingdom of God Is for Losers." I was the songleader that morning and was at a loss to find an appropriate hymn to respond to the sermon. Afterwards, Matt suggested that I write a "hymn for losers." The first line of this text set the tone for the rest—simply using the word "losers" determines the poetic diction. I followed John Bell's style of using everyday, familiar language, focusing on the concrete rather than the metaphoric. Words like "insurance," "bill," and "illegal" are not often used in hymns. I used the Scottish folk tune DREAM ANGUS as the framework for this text. It wasn't until much later that I was reminded of Ted Turner's comment that "Christianity is a religion for losers."

Text: Adam M. L. Tice, 2006; © 2009, GIA Publications, Inc.
Tune: DREAM ANGUS; Scottish folk song; acc. John L. Bell, b. 1949; © 1993, Iona Community;
 GIA Publications, Inc., agent

Christ, the Victorious

Meter: 88 with alleluias

Christ, the Victorious, conquered death;
no grave could hold his rising breath.
  Sing alleluia, sing alleluia,
  alleluia, alleluia!

Christ burst the chains that bound our grave
and freed the earth he came to save.
  Sing alleluia, sing alleluia,
  alleluia, alleluia!

Free now to live, with Christ we rise!
God's Paschal Lamb brought death's demise!
  Sing alleluia, sing alleluia,
  alleluia, alleluia!

Praise to the Spirit! Praise the Lamb!
Sing praise to God, the great I AM!
  Sing alleluia, sing alleluia,
  alleluia, alleluia!

Text: Adam M. L. Tice, 2006; © 2009, GIA Publications, Inc.

The "Christus Victor" understanding of the atonement emphasizes the victory over the powers of death and the grave. I yoked my Easter text with this energetic Welsh tune when I directed the Bethel Missionary Church choir.

Text: Adam M. L. Tice, 2006; © 2009, GIA Publications, Inc.
Tune: LLEDROD; Welsh tune; *Canaiadau y Cyssegr*, 1839

Come, Join in Mary's Prophet-song

Meter: CMD

Come, join in Mary's prophet-song
  of justice for the earth,
for right outgrows the fiercest wrong,
  revealing human worth—
bound not within the wealth we crave
  or in the arms we bear,
but in the holy sign God gave:
  the image that we share.

The "Peace on earth" which shepherds heard
  is not some fantasy.
The angels sang to greet the Word,
  whose birth is victory.
The maiden Mary, not so mild,
  bore into death's domain
true God, and yet an infant child,
  who over death would reign.

Emmanuel, God-with-us here,
  grows peace where we would dare
to act despite our trembling fear
  and bring God's holy care.
The image God made "Us" to be
  is also borne on "Them."
Christ bids us join our enemy
  to sing war's requiem.

Text: Adam M. L. Tice, 2005; © 2009, GIA Publications, Inc.

I wrote this hymn text just before Christmas in 2005, as four Christian Peacemaker Team members were held hostage in Iraq. Inspired by Fred Kaan's interpretations of the Magnificat, I wanted to link Mary's boldness in bringing Jesus "into death's domain" to the fearless peacemaking of the CPTers. I e-mailed it to a large group of friends as a Christmas message. The president of Associated Mennonite Biblical Seminary, Nelson Kraybill, subsequently forwarded it to over 200 people around the globe. As a result, it was sung in churches across the United States and Canada, and even one in England. It was first printed in *Canadian Mennonite* in January 2006. Mary Oyer introduced it to The Hymn Society in the United States and Canada that summer. SALVATION and RESIGNATION are effective alternate tunes.

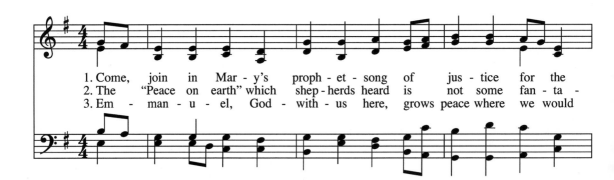

Text: Adam M. L. Tice, 2005; © 2009, GIA Publications, Inc.
Tune: KINGSFOLD; English melody; harm. Ralph Vaughan Williams, 1872–1958

Coming Together for Wine and for Bread

Meter: 10 10 10 10

Coming together for wine and for bread,
tasting the story and hearing it read,
  knowing our hunger and sharing the meal
  opens our eyes to see Jesus is real.

Who will be hungry if, hearing the call,
we offer seats at our banquet to all?
  Who is forgotten? Whom will we ignore?
  Who is the outcast that knocks at our door?

Here at this table, we're welcomed by name;
all are invited, each seat is the same.
  Serving, receiving, and eating the feast
  humbles the haughty and honors the least.

Blessing this table the Spirit is here
granting us vision, so suddenly clear:
  sharing and serving, the body is fed,
  nourished by Jesus, the Wine and the Bread.

Text: Adam M. L. Tice, 2004; © 2009, GIA Publications, Inc.

When I was part of a communion chapel planning group for a seminary class, Ruth Harder was our group's preacher, and she suggested a focus on the role of vision in the Emmaus story. I wrote the first stanza or two during one of our group meetings.

Creation Is Not Built Upon

Meter: CM

Creation is not built upon
  what people make and praise;
the cosmos holds more mysteries
  than all our mortal ways.

The universe was formed by God
  with wisdom far too grand
for us to comprehend, or grasp
  within a human hand.

And yet, we set our hands to carve
  upon the suff'ring earth
our image as a monument
  to human skill and worth.

If we destroy this hallowed world
  to fuel imagined need,
we curse the God that made it good
  and idolize our greed.

Text: Adam M. L. Tice, 2005; © 2009, GIA Publications, Inc.

I audited a course called "Job and the Arts," co-taught by Rebecca Slough and Perry Yoder. My intent in auditing was to spend class periods writing hymns inspired by the content. Despite the inspiring nature of the class, I only came up with two texts (the other is "When Job the Great Was Brought to Tears"). This one draws upon God's response to Job's complaint.

Text: Adam M. L. Tice, 2005; © 2009, GIA Publications, Inc.
Tune: MORNING SONG; Wyeth's *Repository of Sacred Music*, 1813; harm. Richard Proulx, b. 1937; © 1975, GIA Publications, Inc.

Earth Is Full of Wit and Wisdom

Meter: 8 7 8 7 D

Earth is full of wit and wisdom,
  sounding God's delighted laugh,
from the tiny roly-poly
  to the treetop-tall giraffe.
All creation sings in wonder;
  even rocks and trees rejoice
as they join the ringing chorus:
  echoes of our Maker's voice.

Earth is full of wit and wisdom,
  woven into harmony.
Ev'ry creature has a purpose,
  ev'ry flow'r and bumblebee.
Spider, human, redwood, gecko,
  monkey, chicken, mouse, and snake,
live within a single fabric:
  cloth that only God could make.

Earth is full of wit and wisdom:
  penguin, platypus, and snail,
cactus, sea slug, oak, and algae,
  from the microbe to the whale.
In this great and strange creation,
  with a breath God gives us birth:
born of soil to live as stewards,
  called to love and serve the earth.

Text: Adam M. L. Tice, 2007; © 2009, GIA Publications, Inc.

One of my seminary classmates, Brianne Donaldson, suggested that I write a text about the interconnectedness of life, with humans as a part of the mix rather than being artificially separated from it. When I first visited Hyattsville Mennonite Church in Maryland as a candidate for my current position, a men's quartet performed this for the children of the congregation. They were delighted with the various animals that appear within the song. The second stanza provides the title of this collection.

Every Eye Is Different

Meter: 6 5 6 5 D

Ev'ry eye is diff'rent,
  catching diff'rent light
cast from diff'rent angles,
  giving us our sight.
Seeing diff'rent colors
  paints the world we know,
indistinct or focused,
  as our eyes will show.

Some see with their fingers,
  knowing differently
what those take for granted
  who use eyes to see.
Even with a scripture
  we all hold as true,
each one sees uniquely
  what it says to do.

How are we to worship
  when our neighbor's sight
seems to be in error,
  while our own seems right?
Knowing God created
  ev'ry person's heart,
bearing God's own image
  is a worthy start.

Ev'ry mind is diff'rent,
  made uniquely good—
bearing diff'rent lifetimes,
  not all understood.
Giving thanks for diff'rence,
  seeing gifts in all,
is not wishful thinking,
  but a holy call.

Text: Adam M. L. Tice, 2004; © 2009, GIA Publications, Inc.

Our so-called "young adult" group at Bethel Missionary Church in Goshen, Indiana, was incredibly diverse for a small country church. This text is dedicated to those friends.

39

1. Ev-'ry eye is dif-f'rent, catch-ing dif-f'rent light cast from dif-f'rent an-gles, giv-ing us our sight. See-ing dif-f'rent col-ors paints the world we know, in-dis-tinct or fo-cused, as our eyes will show.

2. Some see with their fin-gers, know-ing dif-f'rent-ly what those take for grant-ed who use eyes to see. E-ven with a scrip-ture we all hold as true, each one sees u-nique-ly what it says to do.

3. How are we to wor-ship when our neigh-bor's sight seems to be in er-ror, while our own seems right? Know-ing God cre-a-ted ev-'ry per-son's heart, bear-ing God's own im-age is a wor-thy start.

4. Ev-'ry mind is dif-f'rent, made u-nique-ly good— bear-ing dif-f'rent life-times, not all un-der-stood. Giv-ing thanks for dif-f'rence, see-ing gifts in all, is not wish-ful think-ing, but a ho-ly call.

Text: Adam M. L. Tice, 2004; © 2009, GIA Publications, Inc.
Tune: CRANHAM; Gustav Holst, 1874–1934

Fill Us with Your Breath

Meter: 5 9 7 5 D

Fill us with your breath
  that the Spirit's inspiration brings:
life that's stronger still than death,
  borne on hov'ring wings.
May we grow to live
  as your body, blessed to move in you,
sent to heal as you forgive,
  making all things new.

Stand among us still—
  with the dawn of peace, the radiant light,
morning song and sparrow's trill
  weaving through the night.
May our spirits rise,
  climbing sunward like a fruitful vine,
drawing heaven from the skies,
  yielding sweet new wine.

Be our living guide;
  let your Spirit be our strength and song;
with the gifts that you provide
  lead where we belong.
May we serve your earth;
  give us grace to make your message clear:
we proclaim the world's new birth—
  God is working here.

Text: Adam M. L. Tice, 2007; © 2009, GIA Publications, Inc.

I wrote this hymn at the request of my classmates for our commencement from Associated Mennonite Biblical Seminary in 2007. We sang this as a response to Professor Alan Kreider's charge to the graduates. I had been looking for an opportunity to write a text for William Rowan's tune, which lent itself quite well to our community's a cappella singing.

God Bestows on Every Sense

Meter: 77 77

God bestows on ev'ry sense
beauty as hope's evidence:
  signs of what the earth will be
  just beyond what we can see.

Catch a fleeting glimpse of grace
in an unexpected place:
  just a taste, the smallest crumb
  of the banquet yet to come.

Vibrant pictures in our dreams,
brushed with crystal color schemes,
  vanish from a waking mind,
  leaving just a trace behind.

In a burnt and blackened field
broken ground begins to yield
  tiny, fragile sprouts of green:
  hints of forests yet unseen.

God makes all creation new,
turning back what people do,
  building up what we destroy,
  singing sorrow into joy.

Text: Adam M. L. Tice, 2005; © 2009, GIA Publications, Inc.

This text rests upon the assumption that creation is not bound for destruction but for redemption. Glimpses of beauty now are just hints of what is to come. I decided to use the word "crystal" in honor of my dear friend, Crystal Kempher. This was first sung at the ground-breaking ceremony for the new library at Associated Mennonite Biblical Seminary, the first theological library in America to be designated a "green" building. Mary Oyer led its singing at the Hymn Society of the United States and Canada's annual conference in the summer of 2006.

Text: Adam M. L. Tice, 2005; © 2009, GIA Publications, Inc.
Tune: ORIENTIS PARTIBUS; French melody, 13th c., attr. Pierre de Corbeil; harm. Richard Redhead, 1820–1901

God, Bless the Doctor's Art

Meter: SM

God, bless the doctor's art
 and guide the surgeon's care.
Be with them as they do their part
 to be an answered prayer.

God, speed recovery
 and let this time be blest.
Let hope and faith combine to be
 a source of healing rest.

Text: Adam M. L. Tice, 2004; © 2009, GIA Publications, Inc.

In June of 2004, Mennonite hymnologist Mary Oyer and my sister-in-law Mindie Tice both underwent surgery. I wrote this text to recognize the role of medical practitioners in healing.

Text: Adam M. L. Tice, 2004; © 2009, GIA Publications, Inc.
Tune: SOUTHWELL; Damon's *Psalmes*, 1579

God, Grant This Suffering Soul Release

Meter: LM

God, grant this suff'ring soul release;
  with love inspire the final breath,
and give your faithful servant peace,
  free from earth's pain in timely death.

Into your open hands receive
  this spirit, as the body dies.
Grant us the grace to freely grieve
  as we now loose our former ties.

God, help us all complete this race,
  to live so when our course is run,
when we at last reach your embrace,
  we too will hear you say, "Well done."

Alternate version of verses 1 and 2
for use at a funeral:

God, give your faithful servant peace;
  you have inspired the final breath.
You grant the suff'ring soul release,
  free from earth's pain in timely death.

Into your open hands receive
  this spirit, for the body dies.
Grant us the grace to freely grieve
  as we now loose our former ties.

Text: Adam M. L. Tice, 2005; © 2009, GIA Publications, Inc.

I wrote this for my family as my grandfather, Monroe Tice, approached death. I revised it for singing at his funeral a few weeks later. We sang it with the tune HAMBURG.

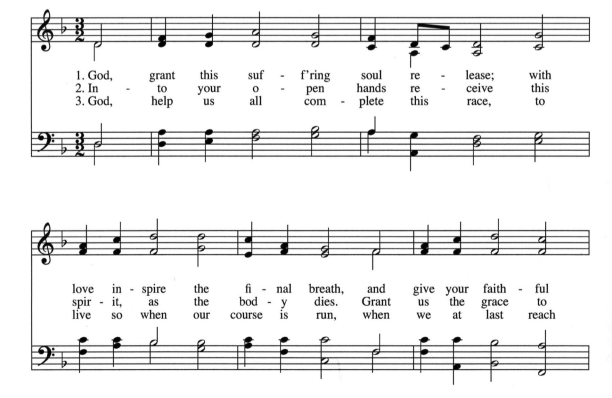

Funeral Version

Text: Adam M. L. Tice, 2005; © 2009, GIA Publications, Inc.
Tune: DISTRESS; *The Southern Harmony*, 1835

God, in Our Praying

Meter: 5 6 8 5 5 8

God, in our praying,
do we hear you calling?
  Are you the source of our desire?
Move us with wisdom,
live in our longing,
  and fill us with your Spirit's fire.

God, in our praying,
do we join your singing?
  Are you the pulse of all we do?
Tune us to justice,
lead us in loving,
  keep us in harmony with you.

Text: Adam M. L. Tice, 2007; © 2009, GIA Publications, Inc.

I wrote this text at the request of Janeen Bertsche Johnson. She wanted a hymn of discernment for use at denominational business meetings at the Mennonite Church USA convention in San Jose, California, in July 2007.

Text: Adam M. L. Tice, 2007; © 2009, GIA Publications, Inc.
Tune: ST. ELIZABETH; *Schlesische Volkslieder*, 1842; arr. Richard Storrs Willis, 1819–1900

God of Music, Guide Our Song

Meter: 7 7 7 7

God of music, guide our song;
  move within each beating heart.
Make our singing pure and strong;
  fill each voice, in ev'ry part.

Sing, O God, so we can hear!
  Make your guiding presence known.
In our confidence and fear
  let us never sing alone.

We are called to sing and shout—
  joining all creation's cry—
psalms that voice our trust and doubt
  as we groan, or laugh, or sigh.

God of music, be our song:
  melody and harmony.
This is where our hearts belong:
  lifted, singing constantly.

Text: Adam M. L. Tice, 2004; © 2009, GIA Publications, Inc.

This is dedicated to the Associated Mennonite Biblical Seminary Ensemble, a choir that I had the privilege to direct for a semester. FREUEN WIR UNS ALL IN EIN works quite well as an alternate tune.

Text: Adam M. L. Tice, 2004; © 2009, GIA Publications, Inc.
Tune: CANTERBURY; Orlando Gibbons, 1583–1625

God Says, "I Give My Earth to You"

Meter: LM

God says, "I give my earth to you;
its future rests in what you do."
 But we, though born of God's life-breath,
 turn earth into the realm of death.

God says, "I give my law as trust,
that you will choose what's good and just."
 But we, who by God's law are free,
 enslave ourselves to tyranny.

God says, "I give to you my Word:
my Son, in whom my voice is heard."
 But we cry out with "Crucify!"
 demanding that God's Son must die.

Christ says, "I rise again, and live,
and my own death I now forgive."
 And we receive a choice to face:
 will we accept this gift of grace?

Text: Adam M. L. Tice, 2007; © 2009, GIA Publications, Inc.

To borrow from Stephen Hawking, this is "A brief history of time." Alternate tunes include O WALY WALY, KEDRON, and ST. CROSS.

Text: Adam M. L. Tice, 2007; © 2009, GIA Publications, Inc.
Tune: DEUS TUORUM MILITUM; *Grenoble Antiphoner*, 1753; harm. Basil Harwood, 1859–1949; © The Late Dr. Basil Harwood Settlement Trust

God, Your Knowing Eye Can See

Meter: 7 7 7 7 7 7

God, your knowing eye can see
  how we use the gifts you gave:
earth and all that it can be,
  which we slash and burn and pave;
and the people you create
whom we persecute and hate.

Woe to us with earthly wealth,
  wasting money, land, and food,
thinking we deserve our health
  more than those whom we exclude:
those who struggle just to live;
those who need what we could give.

Blest are those we see as poor,
  meek and hungry, those who mourn.
Blest are those whom we ignore,
  those we mock, and those we scorn.
Blest are we when making peace,
causing all our wars to cease.

Give us eyes to see the blest;
  give us ears to hear their cry.
Let us give the weary rest;
  let us comfort those who die.
Help us help each other live,
using all the gifts you give.

Text: Adam M. L. Tice, 2004; © 2009, GIA Publications, Inc.

Inspired by Fred Kaan's use of contemporary language and prophetic imagery, this text is based on the "blessings and woes" in Luke 6.

Text: Adam M. L. Tice, 2004; © 2009 GIA Publications, Inc.
Tune: CÂMARA; Chris Ángel, b. 1976; © 2009 GIA Publications, Inc.

I AM the Living Water

Meter: 13 13 13 13 13 13

I AM the living Water
 that cools your thirsting soul.
I AM the Bread of heaven
 that makes your living full.
I AM the Light to guide you:
 I give you heaven's sight.
I AM the gentle Shepherd
 who guards you in the night.
I AM the Vine in season:
 my wine will fill your cup.
I AM the Resurrection,
 and I will raise you up.

Text: Adam M. L. Tice, 2006; © 2009, GIA Publications, Inc.

Teaching a course on the gospel of John, Professor Willard Swartley (now retired from Associated Mennonite Biblical Seminary) drew his students' attention to Jesus' various uses of his identification as "I AM." I wrote this text in just a few minutes in response to one of Swartley's handouts. Chris Ángel named this tune in Swartley's honor.

Text: Adam M. L. Tice, 2006; © 2009, GIA Publications, Inc.
Tune: SWARTLEY; Chris Ángel, b. 1976; © 2009, GIA Publications, Inc.

"I Have No Room"

Meter: LM with refrain

"I have no room, no place to sleep,
within this busy inn I keep.
  But this I have, and this I give:
  the stable where the cattle live."
Innkeeper, did you hear the song?
  Gloria, gloria!
Did you lie sleepless all night long?
  In excelsis Deo!

"What can I do but watch the sheep?
We have a hundred here to keep!
  So I will stay out in the wild
  and send my friends to see the child."
Good shepherd, did you hear the song?
  Gloria, gloria!
Did you lie sleepless all night long?
  In excelsis Deo!

"I lie awake in troubled fear,
in case some foe is coming near.
  I must make sure my throne will stand
  so all will dread my mighty hand."
King Herod, did you hear the song?
  Gloria, gloria!
Did you lie sleepless all night long?
  In excelsis Deo!

"I understand a worker's tools,
but now, there are no simple rules.
  I'm called to raise a baby boy.
  I've never felt such fear or joy."
Dear Joseph, did you hear the song?
  Gloria, gloria!
Did you lie sleepless all night long?
  In excelsis Deo!

"My darling Jesus, go to sleep.
The night is late, the dark is deep.
  This manger makes a rustic bed
  where you can rest your newborn head."
O Mary, did you hear the song?
  Gloria, gloria!
Did you lie sleepless all night long?
  In excelsis Deo!

Text: Adam M. L. Tice, 2004; © 2009, GIA Publications, Inc.

This text graced the back of the 2004 Christmas letter sent by my wife and me. The first four lines of each stanza may be sung by a soloist, with the congregation joining for the final four. It was premiered that same December with the tune presented here, both at the Associated Mennonite Biblical Seminary in Elkhart, Indiana, and St. Patrick's Catholic Church, Urbana, Illinois, where the composer was music director.

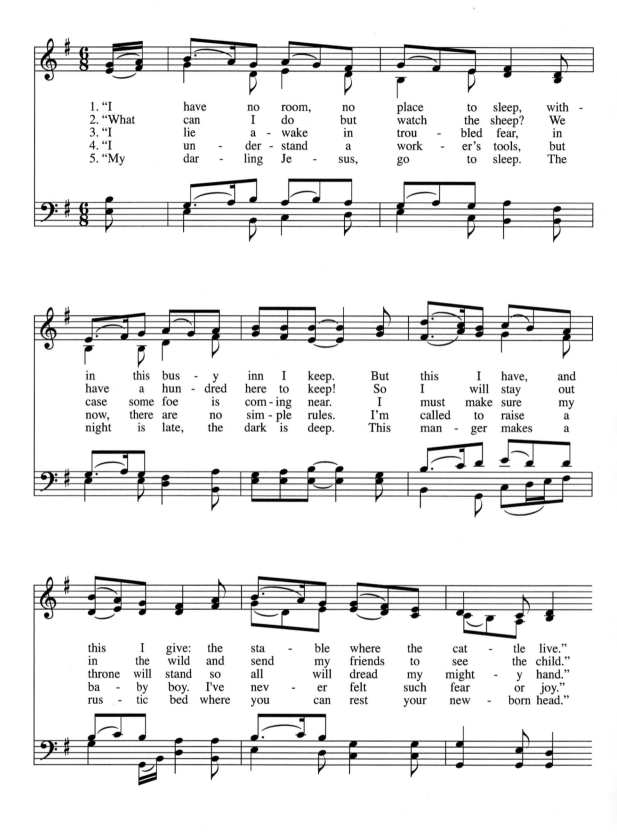

Text: Adam M. L. Tice, 2004; © 2009, GIA Publications, Inc.
Tune: MADRUGADA; Chris Ángel, b. 1976, arr. Chris Ángel and Adam M. L. Tice; © 2009, GIA Publications, Inc.

In Floods of Chaos

Meter: LM

In floods of chaos, seas of grief,
  loud rushing wind, and pounding waves,
will waters drown our sure belief
  that, in disaster, Jesus saves?

When with one voice the people cry,
  but no one hears the poor and meek,
can we believe—as children die—
  that God is strong when we are weak?

If in the comfort of our ease
  we sit and watch the chaos grow,
ignoring desp'rate cries and pleas,
  who is this God we claim to know?

Where charity and love are found,
  there God will also always be.
Love such as this cannot be drowned
  by any storm or crashing sea.

Text: Adam M. L. Tice, 2005; © 2009, GIA Publications, Inc.

I wrote this in response to the devastation of Hurricanes Katrina and Rita in 2005. Stanza four is based on "Ubi caritas et amor" and Song of Songs 8:7a.

61

Text: Adam M. L. Tice, 2005; © 2009, GIA Publications, Inc.
Tune: KEDRON; Elkanah Kelsay Dare, 1782–1826; *The Southern Harmony*, 1835

In the Darkness of the Morning

Meter: 8 7 8 7

In the darkness of the morning,
  just before the hint of dawn,
Mary Magdalene discovered
  Jesus Christ, her friend, was gone.

Days before, she faced his suff'ring;
  she stayed with him as he died.
Seeing now his tomb was empty,
  she remained outside and cried.

As she wept the warmth of sunrise
  filled the waiting world with light.
Then she turned and saw a stranger,
  though her tears obscured her sight.

Asked the man, "Why are you weeping?"
  in a voice she vaguely knew.
"He is gone, and I must find him,"
  she replied as morning grew.

"Mary!" said the smiling stranger
  as her vision was restored.
She cried "Teacher!" and she touched him:
  Jesus Christ, her risen Lord.

Text: Adam M. L. Tice, 2004; © 2009, GIA Publications, Inc.

The moving Easter encounter between Mary Magdalene and Jesus demonstrates the importance of women in Jesus' life and ministry. He chose Mary as the first witness to his resurrection. This hymn is based on the account found in the Gospel of John.

Text: Adam M. L. Tice, 2004; © 2009, GIA Publications, Inc.
Tune: KAS DZIEDAJA; Latvian folk melody; acc. Robert J. Batastini, b. 1942; © 1995, GIA Publications, Inc.

Jesus Entered Egypt

Meter: 6 5 6 5 D

Jesus entered Egypt
  fleeing Herod's hand,
living as an alien
  in a foreign land.
Far from home and country
  with his family,
was there room and welcome
  for this refugee?

Jesus was a migrant
  living as a guest
with the friends and strangers
  who could offer rest.
Do we hold wealth lightly
  so that we can share
shelter with the homeless,
  and abundant care?

Jesus crosses borders
  with the wand'ring poor,
searching for a refuge,
  for an open door.
Do our words and actions
  answer Jesus' plea:
"Give the lowly welcome,
  and you welcome me"?

Text: Adam M. L. Tice, 2007; © 2009, GIA Publications, Inc.

While humans divide the earth according to political ideology, economic expediency, military strength and resource exploitation, God is no respecter of borders. All of the earth belongs to God, and such things as race and nationality should not interfere with our imperative to care for "the least of these." This Epiphany text was an entry in a competition sponsored by The Hymn Society in the United States and Canada.

Jesus Promises Communion

Meter: 8 7 8 7 D

Jesus promises communion
  so that we might live as one,
blessed within the great reunion
  in the body of God's Son.
Taste and see with one another
  bread of life and cup of joy;
we are called to love each other,
  building up what sins destroy.

Holy Spirit, come delight us
  with a taste of heaven's peace;
in this Eucharist unite us
  as our lonely hungers cease.
Bring together all who wander
  from the feast you consecrate,
and restore that grace we squander
  with divisions we create.

God, we offer our thanksgiving
  for the gift of common creed;
and the Gospel way of living
  forming faith in word and deed.
For we share this holy vision
  where your Church can sing "Amen":
Christ, who died and now is risen,
  lives in us and comes again.

Text: Adam M. L. Tice, 2006; © 2009, GIA Publications, Inc.

In 2006 the National Association of Pastoral Musicians (a Roman Catholic organization) sponsored a Communion hymn competition. They sought texts inspired by Jesus' phrase "that all may be one." This text looks forward to a future of full unity at the Lord's Supper.

Text: Adam M. L. Tice, 2006; © 2009, GIA Publications, Inc.
Tune: IN BABILONE; *Oude en Nieuwe Hollanste Boeren lities*, ca. 1710

Jesus Said to Pray, "Our Father"

Meter: 8 7 8 7 D

Jesus said to pray, "Our Father,"
　giving us a name to bear:
children of the Great Creator,
　infinite in love and care.
As a father, arms wide open,
　runs to meet a rebel child
now returned with spirit broken,
　God restores what sin defiled.

Fathers who abuse and frighten,
　or neglect their children's needs,
twist God's image to distortion
　through their hurtful words and deeds.
Fathers who inspire their children,
　guiding them with gentle grace,
show their pride and firm affection,
　giving form to God's embrace.

More than any earthly parent,
　God knows all our hopes and fears,
thrills to see us use our talent,
　feels our wounds and shares our tears.
God, beyond all human naming,
　yet by Jesus known and named
as "Our Father," hear the praying
　of the children you have claimed.

Text: Adam M. L. Tice, 2006; © 2009, GIA Publications, Inc.

This text was suggested/inspired by Professor Alan Kreider at Associated Mennonite Biblical Seminary. I generally insist upon inclusive language, but Kreider prompted me to consider "reclaiming" the image of God as Father. I have attempted to use biblical "father" language, while acknowledging some of the problems of patriarchy. As such, "Father" is presented as an image or sign for God (which can be distorted by human sin) rather than as a definition of God. In this way it is akin to Jean Janzen's "Mothering God."

Text: Adam M. L. Tice, 2006; © 2009, GIA Publications, Inc.
Tune: EBENEZER; Thomas J. Williams, 1869–1944

Jesus, Show Us How to Pray

Meter: 7 7 7 7

Jesus, show us how to pray,
  facing times that numb and stun.
Are there any words to say?
  "Not my will but yours be done."

When we ask our angry "why"
  when our tears have just begun,
still, as you have prayed, we cry,
  "Not my will but yours be done!"

When our hopes are hollowed out,
  all our prayers roll into one,
filled with fear and nagging doubt:
  "Not my will but yours be done!"

God, our hope is out of reach.
  Hear us, as you heard your Son!
We know you respond to each
  "Not my will but yours be done."

Text: Adam M. L. Tice, 2004; © 2009, GIA Publications, Inc.

I wrote this for my friend Niesha Walker, who was going through troubling times. Hymnologist William Smith says that this hymn, along with Dietrich Bonhoeffer's "By Gracious Powers" (translated by Fred Pratt Green) are the only two that he could find from the past one hundred years dealing with the theme of submission to God. This claim was made in Smith's discussion group "The Doctrine of Divine Providence in Psalms and Hymns" at The Hymn Society in the United States and Canada's annual conference in 2004.

Text: Adam M. L. Tice, 2004; © 2009, GIA Publications, Inc.
Tune: HEINLEIN; attr. Martin Herbst, 1654–1681; harm. William Henry Monk, 1823–1889

On the Sabbath Day of Rest

Meter: 7 7 7 7 D

On the Sabbath day of rest
  Jesus broke the law and healed.
Those in pain, he touched and blessed;
  through him wholeness was revealed.
Citing what the law entails,
  righteous leaders called him "fraud."
Jesus taught that love prevails;
  healing is the work of God.

At the margins of belief,
  out of legal order's sight,
to the people veiled in grief
  Jesus shines a healing light.
Rulers meet the dazzling blaze,
  close their eyes and turn in shame
as the lowly stand and gaze
  into Christ's life-giving flame.

God, within these shadow lands
  governed by the law of fear,
let our weary, stubborn hands
  work your justice, even here.
Pour through this abysmal deep
  brilliant light in shimm'ring streams.
Wake us from our shallow sleep
  into grace beyond our dreams.

Text: Adam M. L. Tice, 2008; © 2009, GIA Publications, Inc.

This reflection on Jesus' act of civil disobedience was written for and first sung at University Mennonite Church in State College, Pennsylvania, and Hyattsville Mennonite Church in Maryland.

Text: Adam M. L. Tice, 2008; © 2009, GIA Publications, Inc.
Tune: ABERYSTWYTH; Joseph Parry, 1841–1903

Open Your Eyes to the Image of God

Meter: 10 5 6 10 6 5 7

Open your eyes to the image of God.
Look around and find
Christ's body in our midst.
Open your eyes to the image of God:
body, soul, and spirit,
made whole and holy,
born in the image of God.

Open your ears to the singing of God.
Listen to the voice:
God's Spirit in our song.
Open your ears to the singing of God:
breathing, rising voices,
made whole and holy,
born in the image of God.

Open your hands to the healing of God.
Stand on holy ground:
creation born anew.
Open your hands to the healing of God:
life and love and being,
made whole and holy,
born in the image of God.

Text: Adam M. L. Tice, 2007; © 2009, GIA Publications, Inc.

Our individual bodies are formed in God's image. In turn, these bodies corporately form the active and lively body of Christ in the world. The senses are a means of tangibly experiencing and enacting God's good work. My thanks to Sally Ann Morris for composing WENDY for these words.

"Peace Be with You!"

Meter: 7 7 7 7 D

"Peace be with you!" Jesus said,
  and displayed his hands and side:
Friday's dreadful wounds that bled
  as upon the cross he died.
Now and through all time he stands
  where his true disciples meet,
holding out his wounded hands:
  Sunday's signs of death's defeat.

"Peace be with you!" Jesus said;
  "I send you as God sends me:
rising from among the dead,
  live to set creation free."
Then he breathed upon his friends,
  and the Spirit moved within
with authority God sends:
  power, even over sin.

"Peace be with you!" Hear the call:
  new creation is begun!
Ev'ry creature, great and small,
  lift your hearts to God as one.
Earth and cosmos, raise your voice,
  ev'rything that draws a breath,
sing and dance with God! Rejoice!
  Christ has conquered sin and death!

Text: Adam M. L. Tice, 2007; © 2009, GIA Publications, Inc.

This text was written for a service at Pleasant Oaks Mennonite Church, Middlebury, Indiana, where I preached and led singing the first Sunday after Easter 2007. It is based on John 20:19–31, the lectionary-appointed gospel reading for the day, with overtones of Psalm 150 and Revelation 4:1–8.

Text: Adam M. L. Tice, 2007; © 2009, GIA Publications, Inc.
Tune: SALZBURG; Jakob Hintze, 1622–1702; harm. J. S. Bach, 1685–1750

She Moves Where She Wishes

Meter: 11 11 11 11

She moves where she wishes, the orchard is hers.
The autumn wind whispers and chills what it stirs.
  As amber and crimson leaves dance with the breeze,
  she tends to her harvest and moves through the trees.

Her song is the light upon shimmering streams.
Her voice is the moon that illumines our dreams.
  Her gaze is the morning that bathes us with light;
  her eyes are the stars of infinity's night.

Her feather-soft footfalls are soundless and sure.
Her movement is melody, seamless and pure.
  She reaches for branches that bend as they bear
  the succulent apples that grow in her care.

She comes to me singing; she comes without haste.
She brings me her apples, and offers a taste.
  Her gift, sweet and sacred, bears seeds that take root
  to make me her apple tree, laden with fruit.

Text: Adam M. L. Tice, 2006; © 2009, GIA Publications, Inc.

I began writing this hymn during a seminary class period. Though it bore no particular relation to the topic of his lecture, Professor David Tripp was nonetheless delighted to have had a part in the process. The text draws upon the various feminine descriptions of Wisdom/Sophia in Proverbs, as well as the poetry of the Song of Songs. It was initially inspired by Sting's song "Fields of Gold." This melody should be sung as freely as possible, with great elasticity.

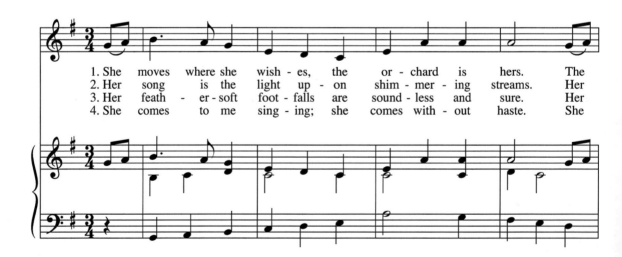

Text: Adam M. L. Tice, 2006; © 2009, GIA Publications, Inc.
Tune: STOWEY; English folk melody; harm. Panel on Worship; © 1998, Church of Scotland

The Church of Christ Cannot Be Bound

Meter: CM

The Church of Christ cannot be bound
  by walls of wood or stone.
Where charity and love are found
  there can the Church be known.

True faith will open up the door
  and step into the street.
True service will seek out the poor
  and ask to wash their feet.

True love will not sit idly by
  when justice is denied.
True mercy hears the homeless cry
  and welcomes them inside.

If what we have we freely share
  to meet our neighbor's need,
then we extend the Spirit's care
  through ev'ry selfless deed.

The Church of Christ cannot be bound
  by walls of wood or stone.
Where charity and love are found,
  there can the Church be known.

Text: Adam M. L. Tice, 2005; © 2005, GIA Publications, Inc.

This text won the 2005 Macalester Plymouth United Church hymn-writing competition. The contest called for texts dealing with poverty and homelessness. My text was inspired by the following quotations:

> True evangelical faith cannot lie dormant. It clothes the naked, it feeds the hungry, it comforts the sorrowful, it shelters the destitute and it serves those who harm it. It binds up that which is wounded. It has become all things to all people.
>
> —Menno Simons
> *Why I Do Not Cease Teaching and Writing*, 1539

> Ubi caritas et amor, Deus ibi est.
> (Where there are charity and love, God is there.)
>
> —Anonymous, 9th c. Latin

Text: Adam M. L. Tice, 2005; © 2005, GIA Publications, Inc.
Tune: McKEE; African American spiritual; adapt. Harry T. Burleigh, 1866–1949

The Dazzle of Diamonds

Meter: 11 8 11 8 D

The dazzle of diamonds in brilliant array,
  the glitter of purified gold,
the emerald feathers that peacocks display,
  and moments of joy that these hold
will falter in time, and their mem'ry will fade
  like dreams that dissolve from the mind.
But search for the beauty that will not degrade:
  the wisdom God calls us to find.

With wisdom of human invention and art
  we seek God with skeptical eyes;
but God is both goal of our quest and its start,
  and wisdom in Christ is the prize.
Find knowledge of God in your body and soul,
  for in these God's image is found.
Seek silence and singing, release and control,
  through movement, expression, and sound.

The world offers wisdom that cannot endure,
  like ash that is tossed by the breeze.
In God, receive wisdom both timeless and pure,
  and grow like the greatest of trees.
Plant wisdom by teaching another to find
  the gifts God has offered to you.
Know wisdom by opening hands, heart, and mind
  to find all creation is new.

Text: Adam M. L. Tice, 2007; © 2009, GIA Publications, Inc.

This hymn was commissioned in honor of my seminary advisor, Rebecca Slough, on the occasion of her installation as Dean of Associated Mennonite Biblical Seminary. It was Rebecca who first introduced me to hymn writing. The theme of the service was wisdom as a priceless treasure.

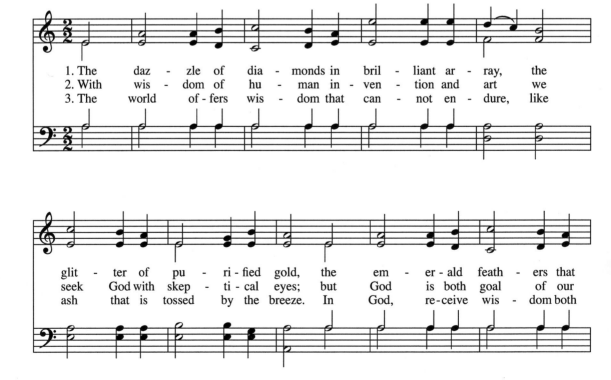

Text: Adam M. L. Tice, 2007; © 2009, GIA Publications, Inc.
Tune: ZION'S PILGRIM; *Christian Lyre*, 1831; harm. J. Harold Moyer, b. 1927; © 1969 Faith and Life Press/Mennonite Publishing House

The First One to Know

Meter: 11 11 11 11 11 11

The first one to know what the Word was to be
was Mary, who welcomed the great mystery.
  Beyond comprehension, she carried her son
  and knew she expected the Savior, the One.
We share with each other the bread and the wine
as once more the earth and the heavens combine.

When Joseph held gently the son of his wife,
he felt the connection of life touching life.
  He cradled a future that he could not see,
  the teacher and guide that this infant would be.
In flesh as a baby, our God came to earth;
redemption is with us, we taste the new birth.

By hearing the story and song of that night
may we, like the shepherds, see Bethlehem's light:
  the Word that created came into its own,
  and first, as a baby, the Savior was known.
So let us respond to the call we have heard
by living and tasting the feast of the Word.

Text: Adam M. L. Tice, 2003; © 2009, GIA Publications, Inc.

One of my earliest texts, this was written for a service of Communion on Christmas Eve at Bethel Missionary Church in Goshen, Indiana. The last two lines of each stanza may be omitted for use when Communion is not celebrated. The accompaniment provided here may also be sung as a four-part harmonization.

Text: Adam M. L. Tice, 2003; © 2009, GIA Publications, Inc.
Tune: SIOBÁN NI LAOGHAIRE; Gaelic; harm. Richard Proulx, b. 1937; © 1975, GIA Publications, Inc.

The Spirit Is a Dove

Meter: SMD

The Spirit is a dove
　with bright and supple wings.
Unseen, she guides us with her love
　and calls us when she sings.
She broods upon the world,
　held soft in her embrace.
She soars through skies with wings unfurled
　in fiery-feathered grace.

The Spirit is a fire
　that purifies and warms.
She flames with love's intense desire
　that constantly transforms.
Our ice-encrusted minds,
　our frozen hands and feet,
she thaws and frees to be refined
　with flames of wind-whipped heat.

The Spirit is a gale
　that blows with cleansing rains.
Before her, pride's pretensions fail,
　and self, laid bare, remains.
The air is sometimes still,
　for none can know her course;
she rises, rushing where she will,
　with world-creating force.

Text: Adam M. L. Tice, 2006; © 2009, GIA Publications, Inc.

Feminine language is not just an expansion of our understanding of God, but also true to the references to the Holy Spirit as found in the Hebrew Bible. Inspired by the poetry of Gerard Manley Hopkins, this text explores three common biblical images of the Spirit.

Text: Adam M. L. Tice, 2006; © 2009, GIA Publications, Inc.
Tune: SPIRITUS COLUMBA; Randall Sensmeier, b. 1948; © 2009, GIA Publications, Inc.

The Strong and Gentle Voice

Meter: SM

The strong and gentle voice,
  the swift, descending Dove,
and Jesus, rising from the stream,
  met joyfully in love.

The Three were found as One
  by Jordan's rugged shore
where John the Baptist preached the way
  of justice for the poor.

And was the Dove content
  by Jordan to remain?
She guided Jesus on to know
  temptation, thirst, and pain.

He faced a three-fold test
  that no one else could bear.
The desert beasts remained with him
  and angels gave him care.

Baptismal waters dry,
  a moment's bliss will fade,
but with the Dove to lead us on
  we need not be afraid.

Text: Adam M. L. Tice, 2005; © 2009, GIA Publications, Inc.

This Trinitarian text highlights the connection between Jesus' baptism and his subsequent temptation in the wilderness. I am particularly fascinated by the note in the Gospel of Mark about wild animals being with Jesus.

Text: Adam M. L. Tice, 2005; © 2009, GIA Publications, Inc.
Tune: FESTAL SONG; William H. Walter, 1825–1893

The World at Day's Dawn

Meter: 5 5 5 5 7 5 5 6

The world at day's dawn
  finds new sounds begun;
the hush of night gone,
  songs rise with the sun.
Creation bursts forth in praise—
  the heavens and earth—
for God tunes our days
  to the song of new birth.

The pulse of sea's shore,
  the steady, soft splash,
the ocean's deep roar,
  and tidal wave's crash,
join with the anthems unheard
  from still, solid ground,
to echo God's Word,
  birthing cosmos through sound.

The city's grand sights,
  the roads, broad and loud,
the frantic bright lights,
  the press of the crowd,
pound out their rhythmic demands,
  chaotic and strong,
forged by our own hands,
  and a part of God's song.

The lamb and the wolf;
  the cow with the bear;
sharp claw and hard hoof,
  each unlikely pair
sings odd duets in the wild
  where mountains rejoice,
led by the small child
  with a strong, gentle voice.

Text: Adam M. L. Tice, 2007; © 2009, GIA Publications, Inc.

I wrote this for my installation as associate pastor at Hyattsville Mennonite Church. I had written a couple of stanzas before moving to Hyattsville from Goshen, Indiana. Upon arriving in the Washington, DC metropolitan area (Hyattsville is "inside the beltway"), I realized that my wilderness imagery required some expansion. Therefore, the third stanza was added to recognize the sounds of urban life. William Rowan's tune provided an attractive framework for my text.

Text: Adam M. L. Tice, 2007; © 2009, GIA Publications, Inc.
Tune: SILKEN WINGS; William P. Rowan, b. 1951; © 2006; admin. GIA Publications, Inc.

This Dreadful Cross

Meter: 8 7 8 7 88 7

This dreadful cross of rough-hewn wood;
 this ring of hammers nailing;
  this barren hill where scoffers stood;
   this stricken mother wailing;
    this veil of darkness as he died;
     this Suff'ring Servant, crucified;
      this broken human body.

This scent of freshly broken bread;
 this sight of wine now flowing;
  this sound, as Jesus' words are said;
   this story, ever growing;
    this taste of unifying grace;
     this flesh, re-formed in God's embrace;
      this rising, holy body.

Text: Adam M. L. Tice, 2007; © 2009, GIA Publications, Inc.

Associated Mennonite Biblical Seminary professor John Rempel requested a text linking the Lord's Supper with Good Friday. I chose to pair my words with AUS TIEFER NOT, composed by Martin Luther for use with Psalm 130 (Out of the Depths), because of the common usage of that tune and psalm within the season of Lent.

Text: Adam M. L. Tice, 2007; © 2009, GIA Publications, Inc.
Tune: AUS TIEFER NOT; attr. Martin Luther, 1483–1546, *Geistliche Gesangk Buchleyn*, 1524, alt.

We Dream of a Turning

Meter: 11 10 13 10 with refrain

We dream of a turning from ages of wrong,
 earth to Eden restored, and our pardon.
Like Eve and Adam, join in a story and a song
 as we wander with God through the garden.

 REFRAIN:
 Where true peace is shining as hate rolls away,
  see, God's bright new creation is gleaming.
 The morning rays that dawn on our weary, waking day
  bring a hope far beyond all our dreaming.

We dream of a feast where there's no one outside,
 turned away due to diff'rence or label,
when all the weapons forged to destroy or to divide
 turn to rust far from God's holy table. *Refrain*

We dream of a mountain where no harm is done,
 where the wolf and the lamb lie together,
a little child shall dance, leading all the creatures on,
 as we join hand to hoof, claw, and feather! *Refrain*

Text: Adam M. L. Tice, 2008; © 2009, GIA Publications, Inc.

One of my favorite Biblical passages is the description of the peaceable kingdom in Isaiah. In Anabaptist theology, God's reign is not just a future hope, but a reality in which we participate. This text both looks forward to the full restoration of creation and celebrates the ways in which the restoration is underway.

What Comfort Can Our Worship Bring

Meter: CM

What comfort can our worship bring
  on bleak and empty days
to those who cannot bear to sing
  when pain is missed in praise?

What sorrow can we dare to own,
  what anger, loss, and fears?
Not just in joy is God made known,
  but also in our tears.

O God, hear ev'ry longing sigh,
  as voices rise and strain,
and meet us in that honest cry
  where praise is voiced in pain.

Text: Adam M. L. Tice, 2005; © 2009, GIA Publications, Inc.

Emily Dickinson wrote that "pain—is missed—in praise." Without the regular practice of lament, worship can tend to omit the reality of suffering in human experience.

Text: Adam M. L. Tice, 2005; © 2009, GIA Publications, Inc.
Tune: MARTYRDOM; Hugh Wilson, 1764–1824

What New Endeavors Will We Dare

Meter: LMD

What new endeavors will we dare
to steward water, soil, and air,
   when thirst for pow'r and warring greed
   drive us to live beyond our need?
Within the ever-changing might
of rushing wind and streams of light,
   God gives us pow'r to change our ways
   and save the earth for future days.

Will changing climate, searing drought,
and melting glaciers end our doubt?
   This web of life we live within
   is vuln'rable to human sin.
Creation groaned as Jesus died:
the planet shook, the heavens cried.
   Yet Love, which sin could not destroy,
   forgives and shakes the earth with joy.

Though still we tear life's web apart,
God weaves again this work of art.
   And if we tear, so must we mend
   and save what God gives us to tend.
Earth yearns for peace that God demands,
and justice grown by human hands.
   As Eden was, yet earth will be:
   God's garden, yielding harmony.

Text: Adam M. L. Tice, 2007; © 2009, GIA Publications, Inc.

Our relationship to creation and our role as stewards requires us to actively protect the environment around us. God will restore creation—we have the opportunity to work alongside God here and now.

Text: Adam M. L. Tice, 2007; © 2009, GIA Publications, Inc.
Tune: RADIANT CITY; Thomas Pavlechko, b. 1962; © 1994, Hope Publishing Company,
   Carol Stream, IL 60188. All rights reserved. Used by permission.

When Anyone Can Buy a Gun

Meter: CMD

When anyone can buy a gun,
 security is lost.
When violent toys are sold as "fun,"
 what clerk will count the cost?
What price is high enough to pay
 when blood is currency?
What body count will clear the way
 to make us safe and free?

When tooth for tooth and eye for eye
 explode to new extremes,
when for each death, ten more must die
 by new, nightmarish schemes,
one hope remains: the Lamb of Peace,
 the slain and risen Lord,
the tortured one, who grants release,
 and breaks the sin-stained sword.

O Lamb of God, you take away
 the sins that scar and kill,
have mercy on us, for we stray
 from doing what you will.
Grant us your peace, and strength to live
 within your victory.
Lead us to love, let us forgive;
 God bless our enemy.

Text: Adam M. L. Tice, 2006; © 2009, GIA Publications, Inc.

I wrote this in response to a series of school shootings, especially the massacre at an Amish school in Lancaster County, Pennsylvania, on October 2, 2006.

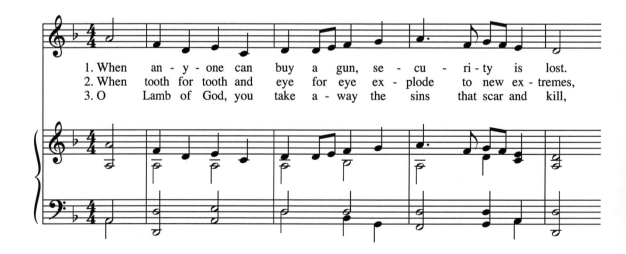

Text: Adam M. L. Tice, 2006; © 2009, GIA Publications, Inc.
Tune: SALVATION; *Kentucky Harmony*, 1816

When Jesus Learned His Friend Had Died

Meter: 88 6 88 6

When Jesus learned his friend had died,
in sympathy and pain he cried,
  though this was not the end.
The people saw that Jesus cared,
but wondered why he had not spared
  the life of his dear friend.

Then Jesus went to see the grave
and, standing there before the cave,
  said, "Take away the stone!"
He prayed to God for all to hear
so that the message would be clear:
  "Through me may God be known!"

"In me you live if you believe;
and those who live in me receive
  my life, though they may die."
Then Jesus called out with a shout,
"Dear Lazarus, my friend, come out!"
  The dead man heard the cry.

When loved ones fall to death's dread sleep,
like Jesus, we can freely weep
  and give our anguished breath.
With Christ, we turn to face the cross
where he confronted pain and loss
  and rose, defeating death.

Text: Adam M. L. Tice, 2003; © 2009, GIA Publications, Inc.

This is one of my earliest texts. The raising of Lazarus is placed at the narrative center of the gospel of John. This event foreshadowed Jesus' own resurrection and provided a motive for the authorities who sought to kill Jesus.

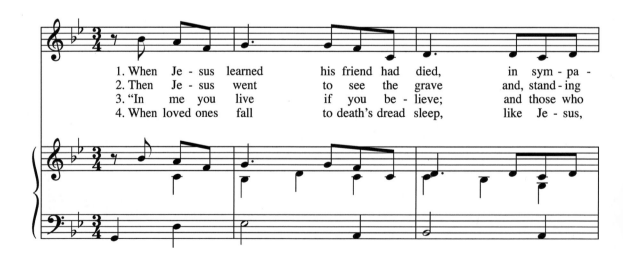

Text: Adam M. L. Tice, 2003; © 2009, GIA Publications, Inc.
Tune: NOEND; Randall Sensmeier, b. 1948; © 2009, GIA Publications, Inc.

When Job the Great Was Brought to Tears

Meter: CMD

When Job the great was brought to tears
  (enough to fill a sea),
he faced a parent's deepest fears
  and cried a painful plea.
"My God, if life is misery,
  why do you give me breath?
Will you persist and torture me,
  or give me peace in death?

Is justice more than we should seek?
  Is God unmoved by pain?
The righteous grow more poor and weak:
  their loss is evil's gain.
O God, restore what you have made
  and make your justice known!
Let evildoers be repaid,
  and leave the good alone."

What can we own before we die?
  A few find pow'r and wealth;
but most, however hard they try,
  lack money, food, and health.
Yet grace is showered like the rain
  (enough to fill a sea),
and we decide, through peace and pain,
  what our response will be.

Text: Adam M. L. Tice, 2005; © 2009, GIA Publications, Inc.

Seeking inspiration for some hymns, I audited a course called "Job and the Arts," co-taught by Rebecca Slough and Perry Yoder. This was one of two resulting texts (the other is "Creation Is Not Built Upon"), and is drawn from Job's complaint to God.

Text: Adam M. L. Tice, 2005; © 2009, GIA Publications, Inc.
Tune: THIRD MODE MELODY; Thomas Tallis, 1505–1585

When My Soul Is Sore and Troubled
Cuando Mi Alma Está Turbada

Meter: 8 8 7

When my soul is sore and troubled,
  when my mind is heavy-burdened,
    then I cry, "My God, my God."

When my voice grows faint from crying,
  when my song is weak and broken,
    then I cry, "My God, my God."

When my muscles burn from straining,
  when my shoulders ache with sorrow,
    then I cry, "My God, my God."

When I know the Spirit listens,
  when I know that Christ cries with me,
    then I sing, "My God, my God."

Cuando mi alma está turbada,
  o mi vida está pesada,
    gritaré, "Oh Dios, mi Dios."

Cuando lágrimas me inundan,
  mi voz y canción se anudan,
    gritaré, "Oh Dios, mi Dios."

Cuando estoy muy agotado(a),
  por la pena abrumado(a),
    gritaré, "Oh Dios, mi Dios."

El Espíritu me escucha,
  y conmigo Cristo llora,
    cantaré, "Oh Dios, mi Dios."

Text: Adam M. L. Tice, 2005; © 2009, GIA Publications, Inc.
Translation: Ronald F. Krisman, 2008; © 2009, GIA Publications, Inc.

"My God!" is an incredibly versatile phrase. Depending on the emphasis and the context, it can express possession and identification, shock, anger, sorrow, and any number of other feelings.

Text: Adam M. L. Tice, 2005, Spanish translation by Ronald F. Krisman, b. 1946, © 2009, GIA Publications, Inc.
Tune: PERILYPOS PSYCHE; Ronald F. Krisman, b. 1946, © 2009, GIA Publications, Inc.

Who Follows Jesus?

Meter: 11 11 11 5

Who follows Jesus? Who will hear his teaching?
Is it the perfect that the Word is reaching?
  Is it the healthy that he has anointed?
  Who is appointed?

We are appointed, we who need his healing.
We need the message, which he is revealing.
  Though far from perfect, we are called by Jesus.
  His calling frees us.

Freed by this calling, this is our thanksgiving:
We sing the myst'ry—Christ, who died, is living!
  There, in the cavern where our God was lying,
  Christ conquered dying.

Christ conquered dying, and his living frees us
if we will choose him, going where he leads us.
  Christ is the vict'ry! Threats of death are hollow.
  So we will follow.

Text: Adam M. L. Tice, 2004; © 2009, GIA Publications, Inc.

This was my first (and, thus far, only) attempt at this rather tricky meter. Note the cyclical relationship between the stanzas and the various stages of faith.

Text: Adam M. L. Tice, 2004; © 2009, GIA Publications, Inc.
Tune: ISTE CONFESSOR; Rouen church melody; setting Carl F. Schalk; © 1969, Concordia Publishing House (www.cph.org).
Used by permission. All rights reserved.

Who Is This Who Breaches Borders

Meter: 88 77 D

Who is this who breaches borders
and subverts the social orders,
  crossing chasms that divide,
  casting race and class aside?
This is Jesus with the broken,
living out what he has spoken:
  "Blest are those who suffer hate;
  woe to those the world calls great."

Who is this who eats with sinners,
calling luckless losers "winners,"
  saying "first shall be the last,"
  choosing feast instead of fast?
This is Jesus, God's anointed,
who proclaims the time appointed
  for the prisoner's release,
  and the jubilee of peace.

Who will worship with the stranger,
off'ring refuge from all danger,
  and invite the last and least
  to the fullness of God's feast?
This is Jesus' body, living
in the simple act of giving
  and the love that we extend
  as a foe becomes our friend.

Text: Adam M. L. Tice, 2007; © 2009, GIA Publications, Inc.

I first heard this tune on a recording and had to dig through my stack of hymnals to locate it. Since it is closely associated with a Marian text, I knew that it was not likely to make its way into Protestant or Anabaptist hymnody without a new set of words. With the keywords "For the least of these," I used The Hymn Society in the United States and Canada's hymn search as an inspiration for this text.

Text: Adam M. L. Tice, 2007; © 2009, GIA Publications, Inc.
Tune: MON DIEU PRÊTE-MOI L'OREILLE; attr. Louis Bourgeois, ca. 1510–1561; harm. Claude Goudimel, 1505–1572, alt.

SCRIPTURAL INDEX

GENESIS
1	Earth Is Full of Wit and Wisdom	36
1:27	Come, Join in Mary's Prophet-song	28
1:27	Every Eye Is Different	38
1:27	Open Your Eyes to the Image of God	74
1:28	What New Endeavors Will We Dare	101
2:4b—3:24	We Dream of a Turning	96
2:15	Earth Is Full of Wit and Wisdom	36

EXODUS
3:14	beyond	18

DEUTERONOMY
10:19	Jesus Entered Egypt	64

JOB
3:1–19	When Job the Great Was Brought to Tears	108
7:1–21	When Job the Great Was Brought to Tears	108
9:2–10	Creation Is Not Built Upon	34
10:1–22	When Job the Great Was Brought to Tears	108
12:7–16	Creation Is Not Built Upon	34
14:1–22	When Job the Great Was Brought to Tears	108
16:20—17:2	When Job the Great Was Brought to Tears	108
21:7–34	When Job the Great Was Brought to Tears	108
24:1–25	When Job the Great Was Brought to Tears	108
28:1–28	The Dazzle of Diamonds	82
30:24–26	When Job the Great Was Brought to Tears	108
31:1–40	When Job the Great Was Brought to Tears	108
38:1—41:34	Creation Is Not Built Upon	34

PSALMS
1	The Dazzle of Diamonds	82
29:3	In Floods of Chaos	60
31:5	God, Grant This Suffering Soul Release	44
34:8	At the Pulpit, Font, and Table	14
34:8	Jesus Promises Communion	66
69:1–3	In Floods of Chaos	60
69:16–15	In Floods of Chaos	60
98:4–9	The World at Day's Dawn	92

PROVERBS
2:1–15	The Dazzle of Diamonds	82
8:1–9:6	She Moves Where She Wishes	78

SONG OF SONGS
8:7a	In Floods of Chaos	60

ISAIAH
2:1–4	We Dream of a Turning	96
7:14	Come, Join in Mary's Prophet-song	28
11:6–9	The World at Day's Dawn	92
11:6–9	We Dream of a Turning	96
44:23	God of Music, Guide Our Song	49
49:13	God of Music, Guide Our Song	49

51:3	We Dream of a Turning	96
51:3	What New Endeavors Will We Dare	101

HOSEA

11:1	Jesus Entered Egypt	64

JONAH

2	In Floods of Chaos	60

ZEPHANIAH

3:14–20	God of Music, Guide Our Song	49

MICAH

6:8	At the Pulpit, Font, and Table	14

MATTHEW

1:23	Come, Join in Mary's Prophet-song	28
2:13–15	Jesus Entered Egypt	64
3:13–4:11	The Strong and Gentle Voice	90
3:16	The Spirit Is a Dove	88
5:3–12	God, Your Knowing Eye Can See	52
5:17–18	God Says, "I Give My Earth to You"	50
5:38–39	When Anyone Can Buy a Gun	104
5:43–45	Come, Join in Mary's Prophet-song	28
6:9	Jesus Said to Pray, "Our Father"	68
6:26	As the Birds of the Air	12
9:10–13	Christ Is for Losers	23
9:12–13	Who Is This Who Breaches Borders	114
12:1–15	On the Sabbath Day of Rest	72
22:1–14	Coming Together for Wine and for Bread	31
22:1–14	Jesus Promises Communion	66
22:1–14	We Dream of a Turning	96
23:13	Christ Is for Losers	23
25:21, 23	God, Grant This Suffering Soul Release	44
25:34–40	Jesus Entered Egypt	64
25:34–40	The Church of Christ Cannot Be Bound	80
25:55–56	In the Darkness of the Morning	62
26:7–13	A Woman Poured Her Jar of Rich Perfume	8
26:26–28	Coming Together for Wine and for Bread	31
26:39	Jesus, Show Us How to Pray	70
27:32–55	This Dreadful Cross	94
27:46	When My Soul Is Sore and Troubled	110
27:46	Who Follows Jesus?	112
27:54	What New Endeavors Will We Dare	101
28:1–10	In the Darkness of the Morning	62

MARK

1:9–11	The Strong and Gentle Voice	90
1:10	The Spirit Is a Dove	88
2:17	Who Is This Who Breaches Borders	114
2:23–3:6	On the Sabbath Day of Rest	72
14:3–9	A Woman Poured Her Jar of Rich Perfume	8
14:22–24	Coming Together for Wine and for Bread	31
14:35–36	Jesus, Show Us How to Pray	70
15:21–41	This Dreadful Cross	94
15:34	When My Soul Is Sore and Troubled	110

15:34	Who Follows Jesus? 112	
15:40–41	In the Darkness of the Morning 62	
16:1–9	In the Darkness of the Morning 62	

LUKE

1:26–56	The First One to Know 85
1:46–55	Come, Join in Mary's Prophet-song 28
2:1–20	The First One to Know 85
2:7	Away in a Manger 16
2:8–14	"I Have No Room" 57
2:8–14	Come, Join in Mary's Prophet-song 28
2:29	God, Grant This Suffering Soul Release 44
3:22	The Spirit Is a Dove 88
4:1–13	The Strong and Gentle Voice 90
5:31–32	Who Is This Who Breaches Borders 114
6:1–11	On the Sabbath Day of Rest 72
6:20–26	God, Your Knowing Eye Can See 52
7:27–50	A Woman Poured Her Jar of Rich Perfume 8
11:2	Jesus Said to Pray, "Our Father" 68
12:24	As the Birds of the Air 12
14:1–6	On the Sabbath Day of Rest 72
14:7–24	Coming Together for Wine and for Bread 31
14:7–24	Jesus Promises Communion 66
14:7–24	We Dream of a Turning 96
15:11–32	Jesus Said to Pray, "Our Father" 68
22:14–23	Coming Together for Wine and for Bread 31
22:44	Jesus, Show Us How to Pray 70
23:26–49	This Dreadful Cross 94
23:46	God, Grant This Suffering Soul Release 44
23:49	In the Darkness of the Morning 62
24:1–10	In the Darkness of the Morning 62
24:30–31	Coming Together for Wine and for Bread 31

JOHN

1:1–5	God Says, "I Give My Earth to You" 50
1:10	The First One to Know 85
1:10–18	God Says, "I Give My Earth to You" 50
1:29	When Anyone Can Buy a Gun 104
1:32	The Spirit Is a Dove 88
3:8	She Moves Where She Wishes 78
3:8	The Spirit Is a Dove 88
4:10–14	I AM the Living Water 54
6:31–35	I AM the Living Water 54
6:35	Coming Together for Wine and for Bread 31
6:48–51	I AM the Living Water 54
7:37–38	I AM the Living Water 54
8:12	I AM the Living Water 54
9:1–41	On the Sabbath Day of Rest 72
9:5	I AM the Living Water 54
10:11–16	I AM the Living Water 54
11:17–44	When Jesus Learned His Friend Had Died 106

11:25–26	I AM the Living Water	54
12:1–7	A Woman Poured Her Jar of Rich Perfume	8
15:1–5	I AM the Living Water	54
17:11, 20–23	Jesus Promises Communion	66
19:16–30	This Dreadful Cross	94
19:25	In the Darkness of the Morning	62
20:1, 11–16	In the Darkness of the Morning	62
20:19–23	Fill Us with Your Breath	40
20:19–31	"Peace Be with You!"	76

ACTS

1:23–26	God, in Our Praying	46
2:1–4	The Spirit Is a Dove	88
2:22–36	God Says, "I Give My Earth to You"	50
24:14–15	God Says, "I Give My Earth to You"	50

ROMANS

3:21–26	God Says, "I Give My Earth to You"	50
6:4–5	Christ, the Victorious	26
8:18–25	God Bestows on Every Sense	42
8:26	An Echo of the Voice of God	10
8:26	What Comfort Can Our Worship Bring	98

1 CORINTHIANS

9:24–25	God, Grant This Suffering Soul Release	44
11:23–26	Coming Together for Wine and for Bread	31
12:9	God, Bless the Doctor's Art	43
15:54–57	Christ, the Victorious	26

EPHESIANS

5:19–20	God of Music, Guide Our Song	49
6:18–20	God, in Our Praying	46

PHILIPPIANS

3:7–11	Christ Is for Losers	23

1 THESSALONIANS

5:16–22	God, in Our Praying	46

2 TIMOTHY

4:6–7	God, Grant This Suffering Soul Release	44

HEBREWS

13:2	Jesus Entered Egypt	64

1 JOHN

3:1–2	Jesus Said to Pray, "Our Father"	68

REVELATION

5:5, 12	When Anyone Can Buy a Gun	104
21:1–5	God Bestows on Every Sense	42

LITURGICAL AND TOPICAL INDEX

BAPTISM
The Strong and Gentle Voice   90

CALL
At the Pulpit, Font, and Table   14
Christ Is for Losers   23
Fill Us with Your Breath   40
God, Grant This Suffering Soul Release   44
God, in Our Praying   46
"Peace Be with You!"   76
She Moves Where She Wishes   78
The Church of Christ Cannot Be Bound   80
What New Endeavors Will We Dare   101
Who Follows Jesus?   112

CHRISTMAS
Away in a Manger   16
Come, Join in Mary's Prophet-song   28
"I Have No Room"   57
The First One to Know   85

COMMUNION
Coming Together for Wine and for Bread   31
I AM the Living Water   54
Jesus Promises Communion   66
The First One to Know   85
This Dreadful Cross   94

COMMUNITY
Coming Together for Wine and for Bread   31
Every Eye Is Different   38
God of Music, Guide Our Song   49
Jesus Promises Communion   66
The Church of Christ Cannot Be Bound   80

COVENANT
God Says, "I Give My Earth to You"   50

CREATION
Creation Is Not Built Upon   34
Earth Is Full of Wit and Wisdom   36
God Bestows on Every Sense   42
God Says, "I Give My Earth to You"   50
The World at Day's Dawn   92
We Dream of a Turning   96
What New Endeavors Will We Dare   101

DEATH
Christ Is for Losers   23
Christ, the Victorious   26
God, Grant This Suffering Soul Release   44
In Floods of Chaos   60
When Jesus Learned His Friend Had Died   106
When Job the Great Was Brought to Tears   108

DISASTER
In Floods of Chaos   60

DISCERNMENT
God, in Our Praying   46

DISCIPLESHIP
Fill Us with Your Breath   40
Who Follows Jesus?   112

DISSENT
Every Eye Is Different   38

EASTER
Christ Is for Losers   23
Christ, the Victorious   26
Coming Together for Wine and for Bread   31
In the Darkness of the Morning   62
Who Follows Jesus?   112

ENVIRONMENT
Creation Is Not Built Upon   34
Earth Is Full of Wit and Wisdom   36
God Bestows on Every Sense   42
God, Your Knowing Eye Can See   52
What New Endeavors Will We Dare   101

EPIPHANY
Jesus Entered Egypt   64
The Strong and Gentle Voice   90

FAITH
God, in Our Praying   46
In Floods of Chaos   60
The Church of Christ Cannot Be Bound   80
When Job the Great Was Brought to Tears   108
When My Soul Is Sore and Troubled   110

FATHERS
Jesus Said to Pray, "Our Father"   68

FOOTWASHING
A Woman Poured Her Jar of Rich Perfume   8
The Church of Christ Cannot Be Bound   80

FORGIVENESS
When Anyone Can Buy a Gun   104

GOD
beyond   18
Breath of God, Breath of Peace   20
Earth Is Full of Wit and Wisdom   36
God of Music, Guide Our Song   49
God Says, "I Give My Earth to You"   50
Jesus Said to Pray, "Our Father"   68
The Strong and Gentle Voice   90

HEALING
Breath of God, Breath of Peace   20
Christ Is for Losers   23
God, Bless the Doctor's Art   43
God, Grant This Suffering Soul Release   44
On the Sabbath Day of Rest   72
Open Your Eyes to the Image of God   74
When My Soul Is Sore and Troubled   110

HEROD
"I Have No Room" 57
Jesus Entered Egypt 64

HOLY SPIRIT
Breath of God, Breath of Peace 20
Fill Us with Your Breath 40
She Moves Where She Wishes 78
The Spirit Is a Dove 88
The Strong and Gentle Voice 90

HOLY WEEK
A Woman Poured Her Jar of Rich Perfume 8
Jesus, Show Us How to Pray 70
This Dreadful Cross 94
When My Soul Is Sore and Troubled 110
Who Follows Jesus? 112

IMMIGRATION
Christ Is for Losers 23
Jesus Entered Egypt 64
Who Is This Who Breaches Borders 114

JESUS CHRIST
A Woman Poured Her Jar of Rich Perfume 8
As the Birds of the Air 12
Away in a Manger 16
Breath of God, Breath of Peace 20
Christ Is for Losers 23
Christ, the Victorious 26
God Says, "I Give My Earth to You" 50
I AM the Living Water 54
"I Have No Room" 57
In the Darkness of the Morning 62
Jesus Entered Egypt 64
Jesus Promises Communion 66
Jesus, Show Us How to Pray 70
On the Sabbath Day of Rest 72
"Peace Be with You!" 76
The First One to Know 85
The Strong and Gentle Voice 90
This Dreadful Cross 94
When Anyone Can Buy a Gun 104
When Jesus Learned His Friend Had Died 106
Who Follows Jesus? 112
Who Is This Who Breaches Borders 114

JOB
Creation Is Not Built Upon 34
When Job the Great Was Brought to Tears 108

JOSEPH
Away in a Manger 16
"I Have No Room" 57
The First One to Know 85

JUSTICE
As the Birds of the Air 12
Christ Is for Losers 23
Come, Join in Mary's Prophet-song 28
Coming Together for Wine and for Bread 31
God, Your Knowing Eye Can See 52
In Floods of Chaos 60
Jesus Entered Egypt 64
On the Sabbath Day of Rest 72
The Church of Christ Cannot Be Bound 80
What New Endeavors Will We Dare 101
When Job the Great Was Brought to Tears 108
Who Is This Who Breaches Borders 114

LAMENT
An Echo of the Voice of God 10
God, Grant This Suffering Soul Release 44
In Floods of Chaos 60
Jesus, Show Us How to Pray 70
What Comfort Can Our Worship Bring 98
When Jesus Learned His Friend Had Died 106
When Job the Great Was Brought to Tears 108
When My Soul Is Sore and Troubled 110

LAZARUS
When Jesus Learned His Friend Had Died 106

LORD'S PRAYER
Jesus Said to Pray, "Our Father" 68

MARY
Away in a Manger 16
Come, Join in Mary's Prophet-song 28
"I Have No Room" 57
The First One to Know 85
This Dreadful Cross 94

MARY MAGDALENE
In the Darkness of the Morning 62

MEDICAL SCIENCE
Christ Is for Losers 23
God, Bless the Doctor's Art 43
God, Grant This Suffering Soul Release 44

MERCY
The Church of Christ Cannot Be Bound 80

MUSIC
An Echo of the Voice of God 10
God of Music, Guide Our Song 49
Open Your Eyes to the Image of God 74
The World at Day's Dawn 92
What Comfort Can Our Worship Bring 98

NEW EARTH
Earth Is Full of Wit and Wisdom 36
Fill Us with Your Breath 40
God Bestows on Every Sense 42
"Peace Be with You!" 76
We Dream of a Turning 96
What New Endeavors Will We Dare 101

OFFERING
A Woman Poured Her Jar of Rich Perfume 8

ORDINATION
At the Pulpit, Font, and Table 14

PEACE
Come, Join in Mary's Prophet-song 28
God, Your Knowing Eye Can See 52
"Peace Be with You!" 76
We Dream of a Turning 96
What New Endeavors Will We Dare 101
When Anyone Can Buy a Gun 104
Who Is This Who Breaches Borders 114

PENTECOST
Breath of God, Breath of Peace 20
The Spirit Is a Dove 88

PRAYER
An Echo of the Voice of God 10
Breath of God, Breath of Peace 20
God, Bless the Doctor's Art 43
God, Grant This Suffering Soul Release 44
God, in Our Praying 46
God of Music, Guide Our Song 49
Jesus, Show Us How to Pray 70
Open Your Eyes to the Image of God 74
What Comfort Can Our Worship Bring 98
When Job the Great Was Brought to Tears 108
When My Soul Is Sore and Troubled 110

PRODIGAL SON
Jesus Said to Pray, "Our Father" 68

REPENTANCE
God, Your Knowing Eye Can See 52
When Anyone Can Buy a Gun 104

RESURRECTION
Christ Is for Losers 23
Christ, the Victorious 26
God Says, "I Give My Earth to You" 50
I AM the Living Water 54
"Peace Be with You!" 76
This Dreadful Cross 94

SCRIPTURE
Every Eye Is Different 38
God Says, "I Give My Earth to You" 50

SERMON ON THE MOUNT
As the Birds of the Air 12
God, Your Knowing Eye Can See 52

STEWARDSHIP
A Woman Poured Her Jar of Rich Perfume 8
As the Birds of the Air 12
Creation Is Not Built Upon 34
Earth Is Full of Wit and Wisdom 36
God Bestows on Every Sense 42
God Says, "I Give My Earth to You" 50
God, Your Knowing Eye Can See 52
What New Endeavors Will We Dare 101

TEMPTATION
The Strong and Gentle Voice 90

TRINITY
Breath of God, Breath of Peace 20
Christ, the Victorious 26
The Strong and Gentle Voice 90

VIOLENCE
When Anyone Can Buy a Gun 104

WISDOM/SOPHIA
She Moves Where She Wishes 78
The Dazzle of Diamonds 82

WORSHIP
A Woman Poured Her Jar of Rich Perfume 8
An Echo of the Voice of God 10
beyond 18
Breath of God, Breath of Peace 20
Creation Is Not Built Upon 34
Every Eye Is Different 38
God of Music, Guide Our Song 49
Open Your Eyes to the Image of God 74
The World at Day's Dawn 92
What Comfort Can Our Worship Bring 98
When My Soul Is Sore and Troubled 110